From The

Books

Of

The

Geislers

The Color Nature Library
WILD ANIMALS

By
JANE BURTON

Designed by
DAVID GIBBON

Produced by
TED SMART

CRESCENT BOOKS

First published in Great Britain 1977 by Colour Library International Ltd.

Designed by David Gibbon. Produced by Ted Smart.

© Text: Jane Burton. © Illustrations: CLI/Bruce Coleman Ltd.

Colour separations by La Cromolito, Milan, Italy.

Display and Text filmsetting by Focus Photoset, London, England.

Printed and bound by L.E.G.O. Vicenza, Italy.

Published by Crescent Books, a division of Crown Publishers Inc.

Library of Congress Catalogue Card No. 77-18620

CRESCENT 1978

4

INTRODUCTION

There are probably at least one and a half million different kinds of animals in the whole of the animal kingdom. By far the most numerous are the insects, of which there are nearly a million species. There are over 20,000 different fishes, nearly 9,000 birds and 6,000 reptiles. Of mammals there are only about four thousand species, by far the smallest animal group. Yet because many are large in size, the mammals are probably the most familiar animals of all. They are also perhaps more easily understood because many of them look and behave in much the same way as we do; which is not surprising since we ourselves are also mammals.

The mammals are quite distinct from all other groups of animals because they have evolved certain characteristics that are unique in the animal kingdom. They are warm-blooded and usually covered with fur to keep in the warmth; the young are most usually born alive; and the new-born babies are nourished by milk from special glands in the body of the mother.

Not all mammals are covered with fur: the whales and the elephants for instance have hairless skins, but even so still retain a few bristles, a reminder that they were at one stage more hairy than they are now. And not all mammals bring forth their young alive: in Australia there are two sorts of mammals which give birth not to live young but to eggs. These are the Platypus and the Spiny Anteaters or Echidna.

Egg-laying mammals are known as monotremes. Monotreme eggs are large and heavily yolked, contained in soft whitish shells. Echidna usually lay one egg, Platypus two. Platypus eggs are laid in a nest of wet leaves at the end of a long tunnel in a river bank. They are incubated for a little over a week, and when the babies hatch they creep into the mother's pouch where they live and grow for the next four months. Echidna picks up her new-laid egg in her beak and places it in her pouch, where it hatches. Both Platypus and Echidna feed their babies on milk, but they do not have nipples; the milk oozes from specialised sweat glands and the babies drink by lapping it.

Monotremes have other primitive features besides their primitive method of reproduction. They have a reptile-like shoulder girdle, and the shapes of some of their limb bones is reptilian. They also have a cartilaginous cup in the eye, which no other mammal possesses, and a cloaca; that is, one vent instead of the normal two or three openings, which other mammals have for genital, urinary and faecal products. There are other primitive features monotremes share with the reptiles.

From a study of fossils we know that the mammals evolved from early reptiles. Today, the two classes, mammal and reptile are distinct, but about 200 million years ago there existed small shrew-like animals which had some features characteristic of reptiles and some typical of mammals. One of the reptilian features of these earliest mammals was that they laid eggs. From this primitive ancestral stock have evolved the first monotremes and then the other more advanced mammalian orders. Platypus and the Spiny Anteaters are the last survivors of the ancient monotreme order: they are mammalian living fossils.

A hundred million years after the primitive egg-laying mammals had diversified from reptile stock, a new method of mammalian reproduction evolved. It was a distinct advantage on the monotreme method because it gave greater protection to the young at the most critical time of life, the very earliest stages. Now the young were retained for a short while within the female's body before being transferred to a pouch.

Top The Duckbill, Platypus or Duckmole lives a semi-aquatic life in Australia's lakes and streams. It has webbed feet, a barrel shaped body and beaver-like tail. Its 'bill' is a sensitive snout, not horny like a duck's bill, but soft like chamois-leather.

Bottom The Echidna or Spiny Anteater also has a beak-like muzzle which is very sensitive for probing for food. It digs out termites and other insects, and burrows so fast it appears to sink into the ground.

The short gestation plus pouching method of reproduction is still employed today by the second order of mammals, the marsupials. The Red Kangaroo *left*, for instance, has a gestation of about 33 days. Its tiny baby weighs only a fraction of an ounce at birth, and yet is able to climb into its mother's pouch unaided. The only help given by the female is to lick a passage in her fur from cloaca to pouch up which the blind, still-embryonic infant scrambles by hooking with its front claws. If it makes the journey to the pouch safely, it sucks onto a nipple and stays there for some eight months until it emerges as a bouncing, near-independent joey.

Top right The Brush-tailed Opossum feeds on buds and birds' eggs. This is an Australian species, but a few small opossums still live in North and South America.

Centre The Tasmanian Devil is a stocky, meat-eating marsupial with a reputation for a foul temper.

Bottom right The Koala is the best-loved marsupial. It feeds only on the leaves of Eucalyptus trees.

The main feature that distinguishes the marsupials is that the young are born at an early stage of development. This is because marsupials have no placenta through which the embryo can be nourished within the mother's body. However, the vast majority of mammals living today have a placenta and belong to the third mammalian order, the placentals. In all placentals, the young are retained within the mother's body for a long period before birth, giving them maximum protection during the crucial early stages.

Placental mammals are further distinguished from marsupials by several other advanced anatomical features, the most important of which is their larger brains. A big brain gives greater intellectual ability, less rigid behaviour patterns and a sense of curiosity. Combined with a more successful method of reproduction, it gave the placentals advantage over the marsupials. All over the world the more primitive mammals were ousted by the

Left The Tiger, one of the most princely lords of creation.

Top right One of the lesser lords of the earth, the Nine-banded Armadillo. Like the Giant Anteater *bottom* this quaint creature has a tubular mouth and long sticky tongue for mopping up termites and other soft-bodied insects.

superior placentals, until, with a very few exceptions, only marsupials isolated from them on the island continent of Australia survived.

Outside Australia, placentals occupied almost every ecological niche, wherever they could find enough food. This led to a great diversity of species, which we now classify mainly according to their teeth. Modern mammalian teeth have evolved from multi-purpose primitive spikes to specialised tools for dealing with specialised diets: carnivores have carnassials for slicing flesh; rodents have chisel-like incisors for gnawing; herbivores have ridged molars for grinding plant fibres.

Left The Giant Panda, like the Tiger, is a carnivore, but its molars have become flattened like those of a herbivore for grinding the bamboo shoots on which it mainly feeds.

Top right A male Vervet Monkey yawning, not from boredom or tiredness but to intimidate a rival with a display of his long canine teeth.

Bottom right Elephants have the most remarkable teeth of any mammal, quite apart from their tusks. They have only one huge molar in each jaw; as this is worn down, another grows forward to replace it.

The mammals take their name from their most obvious character which they share with no other animal: the females suckle their young for some time after birth, on milk secreted from special mammary glands in their bodies. In everyday speech the words 'mammal' and 'animal' are synonymous, but since 'animal' can also mean any member of the animal kingdom, the term 'mammal', which is zoologically correct, has been used in this text to avoid confusion.

Left The Chimpanzee is nearest to man on the mammalian family tree, both in form and in intelligence. The female has a pregnancy of over eight months, and may suckle her baby for two years or more.

Top right The Mara shares the bleak Patagonian desert coast with nesting Magellanic penguins. The young live together in communal burrows; the female never enters the burrow, but calls her babies out and leads them to a special place for nursing.

Bottom right The Red Deer calf is able to run within hours of birth, but keeps well to cover and at a signal from its mother crouches immobile in the undergrowth. At feeding time the mother calls it to her.

Tropical Rainforest

The richer the vegetation anywhere in the world, the greater the number of animals an environment can support. Plants not only provide food for animals but shelter and protection as well; so the more plants there are in a given area, the more animals can live among them. Deserts, with their very low rainfall, are characterised by a minimum vegetation and tiny fauna. In grassland, many more animals species flourish. Woodland, with bushes and trees as well as low-growing herbs, can support a large fauna that lives at all levels in the vegetation, from the roots up to the highest leaves. But the richest environment of all is the tropical rain forest. Here a constant high temperature, high rainfall and high humidity combine to produce luxuriant vegetation which supports many thousands of animal species of all shapes and sizes.

Southeast Asia

There are three major areas of tropical rain forest in the world: in South America, in Africa, and in Southeast Asia. Of these, the latter is the most richly endowed with all forms of life. Here, in the damp gloom among the creeper-festooned trunks and in the vaulted canopy above, small animals of every kind proliferate. Large mammals are there too, but they are rarer and very secretive.

Largest of all the jungle's inhabitants is the Indian Elephant *top right*. A really big bull may weigh up to four tons, and is the second biggest land animal alive today; only the African Elephant is bigger. Elephants are very fond of water; they will squirt cooling trunkfuls over themselves, and lie down and wallow in it. The Tiger *bottom right* another magnificent jungle animal, also wallows to keep cool in the heat of the day. Unlike most cats, it has no fear of water. It cannot bear excessive heat, and is probably more at home in the snowy wastes of Siberia than in the steamy jungles of Malaysia.

The upper canopy of the forest is the home of the Gibbon *left* an ape highly specialised for swinging through the branches by its hands, which it does with peculiar grace and agility. The very intelligent Orang-utan *middle right* also lives in the trees. It is large and powerful, yet amiable and curious too, and strikingly human in appearance. Now confined to isolated jungle pockets on the islands of Sumatra and Borneo, its existence, like that of all big jungle animals, is threatened.

South American Jungle

The Amazonian rain forest is the largest in the world. The main canopy of trees provides living space high above the ground, while smaller trees, shrubs and creepers offer three-dimensional jig-saws of niches at all levels. Flood-waters from the great river system cover much of the forest floor, so most animals in this dense jungle must be able to fly, climb or swim. Some mammals are specialised for treetop living, others stay near water. The Ocelot *top left*, a medium sized cat, can climb and swim with ease. The big, pig-like Brazilian Tapir cannot climb but dives when disturbed *bottom left;* it can even swim underwater. Its chief enemies are the Jaguar and alligators.

High in the canopy live the monkeys, many different species. Most specialised for high life are the Spider Monkeys *top right* and the related Woolly Monkey *bottom right*. They have long prehensile tails, fifth hands. They can hang from a branch by the tail only, leaving all hands free, or pick fruit and leaves with the tail. Less specialised but still an agile climber is the pretty little Squirrel Monkey *top centre*. Its tail is not prehensile, and it lives in smaller trees at the forest edge.

African High Forest

Africa is the richest of all continents in the variety of its wildlife. Most famous are the game animals of the plains. But the heartland of Africa is equatorial rain forest where giant trees rise to a high canopy, their unbranching trunks bare and the forest floor mainly open. Many smaller mammals are climbers, like the monkeys and the nocturnal Tree Hyrax *top right* whose blood-curdling midnight screams ring through the darkness. Larger animals such as elephant and buffalo have room to move freely, but the elusive Bongo *top centre* prefers the densest parts of the forest. Adults have great spirally-twisted horns which they lay back as they force their way through the thickets. Even rarer and more elusive is the giraffe-like Okapi *bottom right* which lives in the depths of the forest, well camouflaged by its stripes.

The Chimpanzee spends much time in the trees, but descends to the ground to feed, sometimes stealing, from outside the forest, as many grapefruits as it can carry *top left*. The heavier Mountain Gorilla *bottom left* is less arboreal; it is placid, non-aggressive and entirely vegetarian. Of all animals these two great apes are closest to man.

Madagascan Forest

Madagascar has been an isolated island for many millions of years, and so a natural laboratory for evolution. Just as Australia was isolated with its marsupial fauna when it parted company from the other ancient continents, so Madagascar was isolated with ancestral forms when it drifted away from Africa. In both Australia and Madagascar the present-day plants and animals are closer to the ancestral forms which were widespread but have since disappeared from all other parts of the world.

All of Madagascar's mammals are unusual, except for a few which were introduced by the first human settlers two to three thousand years ago. Among the most interesting are the lemurs, small to medium-sized forest-dwelling relatives of the monkeys. Most lemurs are about the size of a cat, but some are tiny mouse-sized creatures; most have a long tail and pointed muzzle. Lemurs mainly come out at night, when they leap about the trees in search of insects, fruit and flower buds to eat. Their front teeth are forward-projecting and comb-like, and are used for scooping out soft fruit as well as for grooming the fur.

Mouse-lemurs, named for their tiny size, are among the smallest of primates; they ping among the branches and make bird-like nests among the foliage. Largest of the lemurs and most monkey-like is Verreaux's Sifaka or Monkey Lemur *right*. Along the ground it leaps bipedally, its arms held high. The Brown Lemur *top left* is most active early in the morning and the evening, leaping with four-footed bounds from tree to tree. The Black Lemur *bottom left* lives in social groups and has a wide vocabulary of contact calls and alarm signals.

Lemurs are in a sense ghosts from the past (the name is from the Latin for 'spectre'). They are unique and irreplaceable yet their forests like all forests the world over, are threatened by the encroachments of man. Fourteen entire species have become extinct in the last one hundred years. Now we can only hope that the very last survivors of a once abundant dynasty of primates can be saved, and that they do not become true ghosts with no living physical reality. Once a species has been lost, it can never be recreated.

Temperate Forests

Once upon a time, the greater part of North America was clothed in forest. Over almost the entire eastern half of the continent spread a great continuous broad-leaved woodland, while in the west was a wide belt of boreal forest composed mainly of evergreens. These forests were the home of a rich fauna, from the Brown Bear *left*, one of the largest land carnivores in the world, down to tiny seed-eaters such as the Deer Mouse *bottom right*. Today, most of the virgin forests have been destroyed, and many of the larger wild animals have been almost totally eliminated. But some of the forests and superb landscapes remain, now saved for posterity in national parks. Some of the animals have recovered their numbers, as their destroyed habitats have been allowed to regenerate. A few animals, such as the Raccoon *top right*, are able to adapt themselves to changing circumstances. They are just as much at home foraging around the backyards and garbage cans of suburbia as they are in the peaceful woodlands. But the majority of forest animals need undisturbed forest if they are to survive in the wild.

Not long ago, geologically speaking, Europe and North America were more closely linked than they are today. This is evidenced by similarities between many of the wild animals of the two continents. Indeed, some species such as Wolf, Beaver and Red Fox range across the two continents. The Brown Bear is found not only in North America (where the largest race is known as the Grizzly) but right across the mountains of Europe and Asia to the Himalayas. Many other North American animals have counterparts in Europe: there is a European and Canadian Lynx, the European Bison is first cousin to the North American Buffalo, and the Red Deer *top right* corresponds to the American Wapiti. The Moose *middle right*, the largest living deer, inhabits well-watered forests in the northern half of the North American continent, while the small European Elk lives in the forests and marshes of Northern Europe and Asia.

These animals are closely related to their opposite numbers but it is unsafe to assume that when animals look alike they are related. The North American Deer Mouse looks very like the European Wood Mouse, but they belong to unrelated rodent families. They are both climbing and hopping woodland seedeaters which have come to look alike because their ways of life are similar.

The continent of Europe is relatively poor in wild life, chiefly because it has endured four great Ice Ages in the last million years. It was once, like North America, covered with extensive forest, but these have largely been felled to make way for farmland.

Virgin temperate forests rival tropical forests in the richness of their habitats. Many of the trees are very tall and stately, and in summer their branches form a continuous green canopy high above the ground. Beneath them in layers come the smaller trees and shrubs, then the herbaceous plants. During the summer there is ample cover even for large animals such as the Black-tailed Deer *bottom right*, but the annual shedding of the leaves brings striking changes in light conditions and shelter to all the animals of the forest. Many animals of the forest give birth to their young in the spring. The Roe Deer doe drops her spotted fawn, or sometimes twins, in some secluded thicket. A fawn is capable of running within hours of birth, but it does not follow its mother. She leaves it lying hidden among the ground cover, motionless and almost invisible in the dappled light and shade. When the doe returns to suckle it, the fawn materialises as if from nowhere at her call *left*.

In winter when snow comes, conditions in the forest can be hard. The Red Fox *top left* pounces on mice and voles beneath the snow, or is quite satisfied with carrion from larger animals too weak to survive the cold and lack of food. The Roe buck browses dry bramble leaves and twigs and berries of Guelder Rose *bottom left*. Roe fawns of the previous spring, that capered among the bluebells, will have lost their spots and grown thick grey winter coats. In conifer plantations the evergreens provide some shelter from the wind. Here the irascible Wild Boar forages *right*, rooting under the snow for anything edible his sensitive snout can discover.

The Mountains of Europe The Last Refuge

During the Ice Ages, the mountains of Europe were covered with glaciers, while the lowland valleys, if not actually filled with ice, endured harsh winter conditions. When the ice sheets melted some of the animals that preferred cold conditions moved up the mountains, while others retreated to more northerly latitudes.

The best-known mammal of the alpine zone is the Ibex or Wild Goat *left*. This is a sure-footed beast adapted to leaping from rock to rock among the cliffs and crags, and subsisting on tussock grass. Once abundant in the mountains of Spain and the Alps, it was hunted almost to extermination by the end of World War II. After the war and under resumed protection in special Ibex sanctuaries, its number rose again.

In the wild mountains the Ibex lives in balance with its environment, as do all wild animals in their natural habitat. But the Ibex is probably the ancestor of the domestic goat, the most destructive animal on earth after man. When man cut down the forests that clothed the lower mountain slopes, his herds of goats prevented regeneration of the trees by nibbling shrubs and seedlings back to the ground. Rain and wind erosion denuded the soil, turning the mountain-sides into barren deserts. The mountains of Greece, Italy and Spain still bear witness to this today.

Other wild animals of the mountains are those that have retreated there in the face of persecution by man. The Scottish Wild Cat *top right* was once widespread in Britain, but is now confined to the highlands of Scotland. In Europe, the chief stronghold of the Wild Cat is the Balkans. Somewhat larger is the Lynx *bottom right*, a bob-tailed cat with tufted ears and very broad feet. Like most members of the cat family both Wild Cat and Lynx are solitary beasts, nocturnal hunters of rodents, rabbits and hares, ground birds and even fish. Their catholic tastes in food brought them into conflict with man very early on as soon as he began to keep domestic stock, for they will take poultry, lambs and kids. The Lynx is especially vulnerable to persecution, for the kittens depend on the mother for at least a year; they do not lose their milk teeth or grow their claws until they are nine months old. If the mother is killed the young cannot even catch small rodents for themselves.

The Rocky Mountains

The mountains of North America are the home of several large and spectacular mountain animals. The Mountain Sheep is the only wild sheep in America, but there are fourteen geographically separate races, including the Thinhorn or Dall Sheep *top right*. During the mating season spectacular jousts take place, especially between the massive-horned Bighorn rams *top left*. Combatants charge each other and collide, heads down, with a terrific bone-jarring impact that can send both reeling. Battles may continue for days with no decisive victory to either ram. Such fights do not seem directly related to breeding; rather they act as releasers of pent-up tensions and aggression.

The Rocky Mountain Goat *bottom right* is a goat-antelope, a goat-like mountain animal capable of running up almost perpendicular cliff faces. It pastures high above the tree line in summer, but winters at lower levels. Its shaggy coat is white year-round.

The Cougar or Mountain Lion *bottom left* is a powerful and athletic big cat that hunts what herbivores it may, goats, sheep or deer, and can drag a carcase three times its own weight.

The Northern Ice Cap

The Arctic region is an ice-covered ocean edged by Eurasia, North America and Greenland. No trees grow there, and summer temperatures do not rise more than ten degrees above freezing. Only low-growing plants such as dwarf willows, sedges, mosses and lichens can grow on ground whose surface thaws only briefly in summer and is frozen solid for the rest of the year. The sea is covered with floating pack-ice and is cold and desolate. But Subarctic waters are warmer and support a rich plankton which is the base of the ecological pyramid at whose apex are the seals, whales and Polar Bear *top left*.

Only during the last two or three million years have ice caps covered the ends of the earth. Few kinds of animals have had time to adapt to a polar existence; most mammals there are those already pre-adapted to living in such a harsh environment.

The Polar Bear is probably the best-known Arctic mammal. It is one of the largest bears, and the most carnivorous, feeding on seals which it stalks as they sleep at the edge of the ice. It is a powerful swimmer and expert diver, and has been seen swimming strongly two hundred miles out from land. In the worst of the winter, Polar Bears hole up and sleep, emerging periodically to feed.

Musk Oxen *bottom left* travel widely in search of food—grasses and other plants which they find by scraping away the snow with their hoofs. They are big enough animals to lay on huge reserves of fat during the summer to fuel them through the winter, and their long matted coats, wind and water-proof, keep them dry and warm.

The Arctic Hare *top right* is also active throughout the winter, on high ground where only thin snow covers the vegetation. It has short ears compared to other hares, to prevent undue loss of body heat; and even the soles of its feet are furry. Both the hare and the Arctic Fox *bottom right* have very dense white fur as a protection from the cold and a camouflage in the snow. In winter, the fox often follows Polar Bears to scavenge scraps from seal kills, or it finds, in rock crevices, the lemmings it caught and cached during the summer.

Arctic Summer

The Reindeer of Northern Europe and the Caribou of North America *bottom left* are regarded by some scientists as varieties of the same animal. They differ from all other deer in that the females also carry antlers. Specialised for cold conditions they have a thick double coat and a hairy muzzle, unlike most other deer that have naked noses. Like other Arctic animals such as the fox and hare they have short ears to reduce the body surface through which heat can be lost. Their hoofs are broad and deeply cleft, and splay out for support on snow; on hard ground they clatter like castanets.

In winter Caribou eat reindeer moss, a kind of bushy lichen which they find by scraping away the snow with their hoofs. In summer they feed on leaves, grass and aquatic plants as well. The herds of the far north make long seasonal migrations over many hundreds of miles from their winter to their summer feeding grounds. They follow well-defined traditional routes, where Eskimos and Indians as well as wolves lie in wait for them.

In the Arctic, the Grey or Timber Wolf *top left* is often white-coated throughout the year, though it may be grey or pale brown. Its life is closely linked with that of the Caribou; in family parties it follows the nomadic herds, hunting down the weak and the straggler. Once widespread over Europe and Asia as well as North America, the Grey Wolf had a range greater than that of any other land mammal. But today, as with all big predators, it has been wiped out except in the wilder and least hospitable parts of its range.

In summer the Arctic Fox *top right* and the Arctic Hare *bottom right* moult out of their very dense white pelts. They grow summer coats of a darker colour, and become as effectively camouflaged when snow has melted as they were in their white winter woollies in the snow.

The spawning run of salmon in the Subarctic summer brings a season of plenty to the carnivores of the north. Even the little foxes will feast on the stranded fish, spent after spawning, while the Brown Bear *centre*, an expert fisherman, wades in and catches the fat ripe fish on their way to the spawning beds.

A Sea of Grasses

In the centre of North America there once extended an almost endless landscape of waving grasses, bounded only by the distant horizon and the sky. Through this grassland sea waded immense herds, thousands strong, of Bison and Pronghorn Antelope, while in extensive 'towns' lived millions of Prairie Dogs. All these animals fed on the grasses and profoundly influenced the physiognomy of the grasslands.

The Bison *left* is a massive, humpbacked ox-like animal weighing as much as two small cars. Once, 50 million individuals roamed the high plains and prairies. But with the coming of European settlers the great Bison massacre began. Organized slaughter backed by modern techniques wiped out vast herds. By 1889 there were 540 individuals left. The Indians that depended on the Bison starved. Only just in time was the Bison rescued from the brink of extinction; herds gradually built up again until there are now several thousand animals living in small herds.

In herds once almost as numerous the Pronghorn Antelope *bottom right* also grazed from Mexico to Canada. This is the only antelope that carries branched horns and sheds their outer sheath annually. A fast runner and great leaper, it speeds away from wolves and other danger. When alarmed the white hairs on its rump stand up, a conspicuous signal as it runs.

The Prairie Dog *top right*, a burrowing ground squirrel, once occurred in countless numbers. One town alone covered 24,000 square miles and contained 400 million Prairie Dogs. Such enormous concentrations of a small animal had as profound an effect on the vegetation as did the grass-mowing herds of huge Bison. Prairie Dogs feed on grasses and other prairie plants, continually cropping them down, also felling any tall inedible plants that might give cover to a lurking predator or obscure the view.

Prairie Dogs have many enemies and are a main link in the prairie food chain. In spite of their early-warning system of look-outs who give barking alarm calls to send all bolting underground if danger is spotted many fall prey to eagles, particularly, and to the resourceful Coyote *middle right*. But Prairie Dog's greatest enemy is man, with whom he comes into conflict over grazing rights. Fortunately, the Coyote continues to flourish in places on the prairies, in spite of every man's hand being against him, turning to carrion and smaller rodents when the Prairie Dogs have gone.

The African Plains

In a few places in East Africa the plains still remain in their original pristine state, unspoilt by modern man. Grass is the most obvious plant of the plains, but there are many different species growing together or in different soil conditions, and also many kinds of different herbs growing among the grasses. For this reason, the grasslands are able to support a wide variety of different herbivorous animals, for though many herbivores graze together in large herds and appear to be eating the same plants, they are often feeding on different plant species or on grass in different stages of growth.

The African plains support not only many species, but also very large numbers of some species. The dominant grazers, from sheer size, are the big ungulates, and these still occur in spectacular concentrations such as no longer exist anywhere else in the world. These great herds of plains game migrate hundreds of miles, following rainfall and taking advantage of the fresh growth of grasses it promotes, and thereby also avoiding over-grazing one area. Smaller ungulates move about over more confined spaces and in lesser herds, often keeping themselves ecologically separate by their preferences for pockets of different types of grassland—swampy or dry, wooded or open—around which the bigger animals graze.

The most numerous grazers of the open plains are the Common Zebra *top left*, Wildebeest *middle left*, Coke's Hartebeest or Kongoni *bottom left* and Topi *centre*. Sometimes they are found in separate bands, at others they graze together in big mixed herds. All may feed on the same grass plant, but at a different stage of growth, so that they do not compete with one another and their effect on the grass is complementary. First the zebras, able to cope with a high throughput of poor quality feed, eat the wiry outer stems, too tough and unnutritious for antelopes. Next Kongonis, with their pointed muzzles, can get at the lower parts of the stems, then the square-muzzled Wildebeests pick the horizontal leaves. Several days after a triple clipping the grass sprouts again, providing greenery for smaller herbivores from Thomson's Gazelles (*page* 51) down to grass-eating mice. In addition, in certain swampy areas Topi eat the oldest dried up grass stems rejected even by zebras, thereby maintaining better grazing for the other species. Full grazing by this variety of herbivores keeps the pasture in optimum condition.

In some districts Buffaloes are the dominant grazing animals. They feed mainly by night, dozing and cudding by day *top right*. Buffalo grazing keeps pasture in good condition, for animals move along in a bunch, nosing beneath the tougher top growth for green shoots underneath, then trampling the old stems into a mulch. Next time the herd grazes that way it will find new growth stimulated by the previous cropping.

In some parts of the African plains the pastoral people have traditionally lit grass fires to burn off the old stems useless to cattle, and to promote the sprouting of fresh shoots. It is thought that annual burning is probably a major factor in maintaining the open plains and preventing encroachment by trees.

Plains game as well as cattle benefit from the new grass. The Warthog *bottom right* grazes almost invisible shoots among the remains of scorched old grass. One of the most grotesque of mammals is a big male Warthog with his knobbly face and wicked curved tusks yet he has a certain appeal, perhaps on account of his pure ugliness. Certainly, his back view as he trots away with tail held straight up is far from lovely, but very comical.

The Hunters of the Plains

The grass-eaters of the African plains are in constant fine balance with the plants of the environment. In just as fine balance with the herbivores are the carnivores. The chief predator of plainsgame is the Lion *bottom left* and its prey is generally the most numerous herbivore on its home range. In some places this may be Buffalo, in others Wildebeest or Common Zebra; it does not show a particular preference for one kind of meat, but just takes whatever it can get most readily.

Lions can and often do hunt by day, but more usually hunt at night. They employ a variety of techniques, sometimes hunting singly, sometimes in groups, stalking the prey by stealth and then with a powerful spurt of speed rushing on it and bowling it over. They do not kill more than they need, and what is left of the carcase provides a living for a variety of other animals. After eating as much as they can hold, lions retire to the shade to doze through the heat of the day.

The Leopard *middle left* is the most secretive of the great African cats. It is usually found in forest or where plains and woodland meet, and takes its prey by leaping on it from an overhanging branch or from an ambush in thick cover.

The Cheetah *right* is the fastest animal on land. It hunts only by day and fetches down even the fastest antelopes by sheer speed. Like the Lion it selects its prey and stalks it for a long time before the final rush. It does not make a kill every time it gives chase; sometimes the dodging antelope or gazelle is able to outrun it and escape. If the Cheetah cannot catch it within a couple of hundred yards it has to give up, exhausted.

Among the medium-sized cats is the Serval *top left*, which like the Leopard lives in bushy country to forests rather than out on completely open grassland. it preys on various small animals from the smaller antelopes and hares down to mice, lizards and ground-nesting birds such as guinea fowl.

The predators of the plains do not kill for sport, but only of necessity. Except in the breeding season when newborn young are taken, the great cats

more often kill male animals in their prime than females or young. There are always more males than are necessary for the breeding stock, and these live solitary lives, driven from the herds by the dominant males. Herd animals have many pairs of eyes, ears and nostrils to detect danger, so may more readily escape than the lone males. The effect of the predators is therefore to reduce the numbers of males. In harem societies like those of zebras and antelopes only a few males are needed to maintain the population. The excess males promote healthy competition and provide food for the carnivores. The carnivores keep herbivore populations stable; plainsgame are capable of population explosions if their numbers are not checked. So the carnivores indirectly protect the habitat, for if herbivores increased unchecked, they would overgraze the plains.

Hunting Dogs *top left* are the most efficient killers and, like the big cats, most of their prey is solitary males. They are nomads rarely staying long anywhere unless rearing small cubs, so the herds are never harassed unduly by them, or over-cropped. Their hunting technique is quite different from that of any of the cats; they are long distance runners with great staying power, and they hunt in co-ordinated packs.

Hunting Dogs hunt by day, but the Spotted Hyena *bottom left* hunts by night. Hyenas are not merely scavengers and parasites, lazy cowardly animals stealing from lions as was once thought. They are also major predators in their own right, efficiently hunting and despatching their prey and leaving hardly a scrap; for hyenas have the most powerful jaws in proportion to their size of any living animal.

All the major carnivores, apart from the hyena, leave some of their kill. This is quickly disposed of by a variety of scavengers: vultures, storks, the hyenas, and the Black-backed Jackal *top right*. Scavengers are an essential part of the ecology of the plains, disposing of the refuse and keeping the place sweet.

Baboons live in troops and travel many miles each day in their search for food, the babies clinging under their mothers' bellies as they go, the older youngsters riding jockey *bottom right*. They eat mainly vegetable food, a lot of grass and whatever new shoots, pods, fallen fruit and so on they can find. They also eat locusts, scorpions and other meat, including, surprisingly, young antelopes which they catch and kill. But they are very inefficient predators, and must themselves be constantly on the watch for their arch-enemy, the Leopard.

At the Waterhole

During the dry season most big animals need to drink every day. Antelopes such as Impala *top left* come to the waterhole during the afternoon and evening, in a close herd. Each animal drinks from the very edge for less than half a minute; usually some remain watchful while others hastily suck. Then they leave the area as quickly as they can, aware that at the waterhole they are specially vulnerable to all kinds of predators, from crocodiles and pythons in the water, to a leopard on an overhanging branch or lioness in the bushes *middle left*. Male lions often do not take their full share of responsibility when it comes to feeding the family, and it is usually the lioness that does the hunting, the lion helping himself later as he pleases. Lionesses will often hunt by concealing themselves near a game track along which they know zebras and antelopes must come to drink. Their tawny coats blend well with the grey twigs and yellow grasses. A single lioness hunting on her own stands a better chance of bringing down her quarry if she can thus launch a surprise attack from close quarters. Sometimes one lioness will deliberately give her scent to panic game into the reaches of other lionesses lurking hidden.

Zebras, like Impala, are very nervous when they come to water, and suck their fill as quickly as they can. Any sudden noise makes them wheel round in alarm; even a harmless Warthog trotting past can cause a sudden momentary panic *bottom left*. In contrast, thirsty lions take their time at the waterhole. Their method of drinking is slow and laborious, and it may take twenty minutes for them to get their fill by lapping.

The Nyala *right* lives in bush country never far from water. The ram is a magnificent beast with long crest and mane shaggier than any other antelope. Females look very different, hornless and bright chestnut red with many white side stripes. They are exclusively browsers, except when grass is young and tender; normally they feed on leaves, pods and fruit.

When an African Elephant comes to water *next page* it can be heard drinking from a long way away. It sucks up water in its trunk and then squirts it into its stomach with a noise like an ancient cistern emptying.

The Giant Pachyderms

Amphibious Hippopotamuses *top right* spend the day wallowing in the water to keep cool and avoid sunburn. They surface to breathe, with much snorting and ear-flicking. For so bulky an animal they can swim surprisingly fast, both at the surface and underwater, where they move along the bottom with extraordinary grace. At night they leave the water to feed, cropping grass with lawn-mower efficiency.

The Black Rhinoceros *bottom right* sometimes rests out in the full sun, dozing in the baking heat of a dust bowl. This rhino, like the elephant, is a browser, eating the leaves and twigs of bushes which it collects with pointed upper lip. The White Rhinoceros, a rarer, larger animal, has a broad, square muzzle and like the hippo crops grass.

It is well-known that hippos, rhinos and elephants are related. Less well known is their little cousin the Rock Hyrax or Dassie *centre*. Hyraxes are small robust animals, somewhat like big guinea pigs, but in spite of their rodent-like outward appearance their teeth prove them to be most closely akin to the elephant.

Browsers of the Bush

The bushlands of Africa are a wilderness of thickets that stretch for many hundreds of square miles. Most of the trees and shrubs are thorny, but in spite of this the animal inhabitants are mainly browsers for the simple reason that grass is often non-existent. Elephant, Black Rhinoceros, Giraffe, Greater and Lesser Kudu, Gerenuk, Impala and Dikdiks are the main inhabitants. They may all eat the same bushes but do not compete with one another because they feed at different levels according to their stature.

Tallest of browsers by reason of its elongated legs and neck is the Giraffe *left*. It has a long prehensile upper lip, and extensible tongue for collecting leaves and twigs *above*. It does not always feed at maximum height but it is the only animal that can reach high foliage without pushing the tree over first.

Nearly as tall as a giraffe is the elephant when reaching up with its dexterous trunk. A most destructive feeder, an elephant will pull down branches or uproot a tree to get at the upper twigs; but smaller animals benefit by having branches brought down to their level.

Like the giraffe, the exceptionally elegant Gerenuk has a very long neck, and it further increases its browsing height by standing upright on its hind legs with its forefeet among the branches *top right*. The Greater Kudu *following page* browses at about the same height as the Gerenuk, but it prefers steep hillsides and rough gullies, whereas the Gerenuk lives in flat country.

Below Gerenuk-level feeds the Black Rhinoceros, and lower still the Impala *centre*. A young buck such as this yearling has spiky horns; mature males have very elegant and characteristic lyre-shaped horns.

Smallest of all the browsers are the dikdiks, tiny, dainty antelopes with spiky horns and a proboscis-like snout. Guenther's Long Snouted Dikdik *bottom right* lives singly or in pairs in very arid bush country and does not drink, obtaining all the moisture it needs from leaves and shoots and fallen fruits. It is mainly nocturnal, yet often appears to be the only mammalian inhabitant of the bush out by day. In spite of its diminutive size it is more conspicuous than many of the bigger animals, which do an almost instant disappearing trick as they melt away into the dense bush.

49

African Stripes

A Greater Kudu bull *left* with his twisted horns, throat fringe and majestic carriage is one of the most magnificent of antelopes. Females generally live in herds, but males are usually solitary. During the heat of the day a bull will rest and chew the cud in the shade of trees, where his white stripes on a grey-brown coat render him almost invisible until a twitching ear or stamping foot gives him away.

The conspicuous black-and-white stripes of the small Thomson's Gazelles serve the opposite purpose to the thin vertical stripes of the Kudu. When alarmed Tommies leap away with spectacular bounds *bottom right*. Their stripes flash as they dash hither and thither, and may have a dazzling effect on a predator such as a lion, confusing it and causing it to miss its aim.

The Roan Antelope *top right* is third largest of African antelopes, after the Eland and Greater Kudu. Its contrasting black and white facial pattern acts as a recognition mark to other members of the species. Its body colour is plain fawn, and both sexes carry backward curving horns. Males are very pugnacious and aggressive, and start fighting when quite young.

Hot Deserts of Africa

The great Sahara desert contains some of the hottest, driest places in the world. But there are degrees of harshness within deserts and in some areas sparse patches of drought resistant vegetation grow. These sprout incredibly quickly after rain and are sought out by the Addax *top left*, a nomadic desert-dwelling antelope. Addax were once plentiful throughout the Sahara, but are now one of the most threatened antelopes, hunted by nomads, oil surveyors and soldiers in motor cars.

Addax do not require free water to drink; they obtain all the moisture they need from their food. All desert animals have physiological devices to help conserve water in their bodies. The Arabian Camel *right* is the best-known animal in this respect. It can go without drinking for many days, and can lose well over a third of its body weight in dehydration. Then, when it drinks it can recoup this loss in just two or three good draughts. To prevent loss of body fluids by sweating, the camel and other desert animals allow their temperatures to rise with the air temperature as much as 9°F without getting feverish.

The Gemsbok *bottom* was formerly found throughout the Kalahari, Karroo and Namib deserts of southern Africa, together with immense herds of Springbok *background*. Both drink water when it is available, but can go without if necessary, eating wild water melons and licking dew for moisture.

The Andes

The Llama *left* is a humpless woolly little camel. It has been domesticated for at least 4000 years by the peoples of the High Andes, and it is still much used as a beast of burden. Its temper is even more uncertain then the camel's, and it readily spits and bites.

The Alpaca *bottom right* was probably also derived from the same wild ancestor as the Llama. It is bred for its very long wool, finer quality than that of any other mammal and once woven into robes for Inca royalty.

The wild relatives of the Llama and Alpaca are the Guañaco and the Vicuña, highly specialised wild camels whose ancestors can be traced back to primitive Eocene predecessors. Like all creatures of the high mountains they have physiological adaptations to enable them to live at very high altitudes. Their hearts are considerably enlarged and their blood can take in more oxygen than that of any other mammal.

The Chinchilla *top right* is another animal of the High Andes renowned and, like the Vicuña, much persecuted for its very fine fur. At the beginning of the century it was trapped to the verge of extinction in the wild, but is now protected by law.

Central Asia

After the retreat of the last Ice Age, the steppes of Asia, like the American prairies and the African plains, supported vast herds of grazing animals. Some are now extinct, such as the Wild Ox and the Tarpan, a wild horse; others, like the Red Deer, survive. The Saiga *top left* was recently numbered in thousands, but slaughtered for its horns, used in medicine by the Chinese. This odd-looking little antelope has a bulbous, highly developed nose, an adaptation for moistening and warming very cold, dry air before breathing it into the lungs. Now stringently protected, its numbers are increasing.

The Snow Leopard or Ounce *right* inhabits treeless mountainous areas of Central Asia, where it preys on wild sheep and goats. Almost nothing is known of its life in the wild.

Absolutely nothing is known of Père David's Deer *bottom left* in the wild. This donkey-shaped deer was discovered by the French missionary and naturalist, Père Armand David in 1865. It was already extinct in the wild, but kept in the walled Imperial Hunting Park near Peking. Luckily living animals as well as dead specimens were brought to Europe; the imperial animals were later killed for meat by soldiers. Now herds exist in many zoos and breeding pairs have been sent back to China.

Wetlands

Marshes are more extensive in tropical countries than they are in temperate regions. In Africa there are many large areas of swamp; the gigantic natural reservoir of the Nile, for instance, has created hundreds of square miles of papyrus-choked wetlands, home of several unusual antelopes, and of the huge amphibious Hippopotamus.

In South America, the wide flood plain of the lower Amazon produces a complex of lakes, inundated forest and marshes. Here lives the largest rodent in the world, the gentle, inoffensive, pig-sized Capybara *top left*. Web-footed though not very streamlined it spends much of its time in the water, sometimes swimming long distances beneath the surface. When undisturbed it comes out on land to feed on the swamp vegetation.

Rhinoceroses have lived in Asia for 50 million years, but today are almost extinct. Here only a very few Sumatran and Javan Rhinoceroses are left, in forest reserves. The Great Indian Rhinoceros *bottom left* is less endangered, but survives only in remote areas of northern India, in waterlogged meadows and swamps. It feeds on grass

shoots and Water Hyacinth plants and its pathways make tunnels through the twelve-foot high elephant grass. Even more than the Saiga's, its horns are thought . by the Chinese to have medicinal and aphrodisiac properties, hence its near extermination. But thanks to effective protection, its numbers have slightly increased recently.

The world of the marshes is an enclosed community beyond which many marsh-dwellers do not venture. The Canadian Otter *top right* is a mammal perfectly adapted to an aquatic life; it hunts frogs, fishes, birds and crayfish in the marshes, but also travels extensively between marshes, by river or overland. An exceptionally playful animal it delights in snow and ice, enjoying toboggan runs and slides until really hard weather forces it to stop fooling about.

The Beaver *bottom right* creates its own wetlands. A natural engineer, it dams streams by felling trees. Canals are dug to float logs to its dams. In the centre of the pond behind the dam it builds a great lodge of branches and twigs, cemented with mud and grass, which acts as home and food store to a pair and their family. At one time beavers were found all across Europe as well as in North America. Now they are one of the rarest of European mammals. Wherever their numbers are very sparse, they tend to live in holes in the river banks and do not build dams and lodges.

The Seafarers

A few mammals that once lived on land have taken to living in the sea. The Californian Sea Lion *left* is one of the eared seals. It is more at home on the land than are the True Seals, as it can bring its hind flippers forward to lumber about. It is common on rocky coasts of California, also on the Galapagos Islands. It lives in large herds, and is inquisitive and intelligent.

The Atlantic Walrus *top right* lives in big herds, resting on coastal beaches and ice floes or grubbing about the sea bed with its tusks for crabs, shellfish and sea urchins which it swallows whole. It also swallows pebbles; it has few teeth, and the pebbles take the place of chewing, crushing the shells in the stomach.

The bull Elephant Seal *bottom right* is a ponderous mountain of flesh, the largest of all seals. He has a large drooping nose which he can inflate to form a big cushion. In the breeding season bulls come ashore and challenge one another with intimidating roars, snorting loudly down their blown up noses.

Ocean-goers

The whales and dolphins have evolved from a group of mammals that went to sea some 70 million years ago. They are highly specialised aquanauts, streamlined and fish-shaped. So completely aquatic are they that they are totally unable to return to land, as do the seals, to give birth to their young. Their order contains the biggest animal the world has ever known, the gigantic Blue Whale, as well as many other leviathans. Since earliest times man has made use of whales, but recent overexploitation has brought many of these marine giants to the brink of extinction.

The Right Whale *top left* was so-called by the old-time whalers because it was the "right" whale to catch. Populations were formerly numbered in tens of thousands; today the remnant is being actively protected by a growing number of whaling nations. Right Whales sometimes breach—that is, leap out of the sea—and crash back amid a storm of spray. This may be a form of play, or a way of announcing themselves to other whales some miles away.

Right Whales are toothless; their mouths have plates of baleen or whalebone with which they sieve small shrimps from the water. Dolphins are small toothed whales. The best known is the Bottle-nosed *right,* the highly intelligent and friendly cetacean so popular at many large aquaria. These dolphins respond well to training, even developing ideas for themselves and initiating new games.

The Bottlenose is usually grey with white belly. Most strikingly coloured of all dolphins is the black and white Commerson's Dolphin *middle left.* Little is known of this species, but it appears to be sociable and playful.

Unrelated to whales and dolphins, but like them entirely aquatic, is the Manatee or Sea Cow *bottom left.* More nearly related to elephants than to any other mammal, Manatees live in warm coastal waters and estuaries, and browse on soft aquatic plants.

There are idealistic laws designed to protect the defenceless Manatee and all the other animals, large and small herbivore or predator, that are in such danger from over-exploitation by man. Let us hope that people everywhere will soon come to regard these laws as sensible and right, for man's own good in the end, as well as for the good of the wild animals. Like all natural predators man too should harvest the resources of the earth to satisfy hunger, not greed.

Jonathan Geisler

INDEX

All photographs supplied by:
Colour Library International Ltd., 80-82, Coombe Road, New Malden, Surrey, England.
and
Bruce Coleman Ltd., 16a-17a, Windsor Street, Uxbridge, Middx, England.